KIRKCALDY & CENTRAL FIFE'S

TRAMS AND BUSES

WALTER BURT

AMBERLEY PUBLISHING

Acknowledgements

For their help in providing photographic images for this book, I must thank Robert Dickson, Paul Redmond, Innes Cameron, Grahame Wareham, Barry Sanjana, Gordon Stirling, Clive A. Brown, Stephen Dowle, Kenneth Barclay, Michael Laing, Suzy Scott, Nelson Ewan, John Sinclair, Allan Morton, Terry Gilley, Bill Dewar and Chris Cuthill.

Dedicated to 'Beanie' Boy - 2012.

ALSO AVAILABLE FROM AMBERLEY PUBLISHING

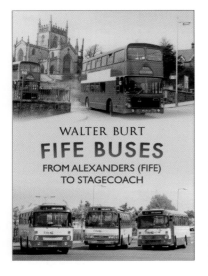

Fife Buses: From Alexanders (Fife) to Stagecoach
Walter Burt

The history of Fife buses from the 1960s to the early 1990s.

978 1 4456 0992 8
96 pages, full colour

First published 2012

Amberley Publishing
The Hill, Stroud
Gloucestershire, GL5 4EP

www.amberley-books.com

Copyright © Walter Burt , 2012

The right of Walter Burt to be identified as the Author of this work has been asserted in accordance with the Copyrights, Designs and Patents Act 1988.

ISBN 978 1 4456 1140 2
EBOOK ISBN 978 1 4456 1164 8

British Library Cataloguing in Publication Data.
A catalogue record for this book is available from the British Library.

Typeset in 9.5pt on 12pt Celeste.
Typesetting by Amberley Publishing.
Printed in the UK.

Introduction

Let us take another step back in time to start our journey through this book, say, just before 1903. Around this time, it was the railways who were the main transport providers, not only in Fife but up and down the length and breadth of the country. This would change with the introduction of the tramway system, followed by the motor bus. In this book we shall have a look at the early trams and motor buses which served in Kirkcaldy and the central Fife area, and see how the tram system developed before its demise in 1932. We will then have a look at the various buses that were introduced to the area and how they developed through time to the modern day vehicles used by Stagecoach in Fife at present.

When browsing through the pages of this book, you may see a lot of changes from the distant, and the not so distant past. I hope that the images rekindle a few memories for the older generation, and introduce a new outlook on the area to the younger generation. I do try hard to research on the history, but I may make a mistake or two, for which I apologise in advance. Early tram images have been found in various picture postcards of the era and other photographs purchased through eBay. A lot of the subject matter has been covered already in other publications and I do not wish to merely repeat what has already been published. I will try and provide a new outlook and perspective on the subject – from the layman's point of view.

Most of the images used within these pages are in colour, but a good few are in black and white, as they are important enough for inclusion in this book. This may be because of a certain location, vehicle type or occasion. My practice when compiling these books is to include both the registration number as well as the fleet numbers of the vehicles in the photographs as vehicles may appear more than once within these pages with a different fleet number or registration.

Brief History

At the turn of the twentieth century, a few horse-drawn buses existed within Kirkcaldy, connecting the various outlying small suburbs such as Dysart, Gallatown and Newtown to the town centre and beyond. They also provided a connection with the town's railway station.

It was Kirkcaldy which had the honour of being the first town in Fife to build a tramway after obtaining Parliamentary Authority to build several lines in the town. The author Wingate H. Bett, when researching Fife's trams in 1940, believed that a horse tramway once existed between Leven and Lundin Links, but was unable to provide any definitive confirmation of this. It would have been nice to have been able to dig deep enough to be able to find out for sure. Kirkcaldy's system opened on 28 February 1903 and connected Gallatown and Linktown (the west end of Link Street), by way of the Path and High Street. This route apparently suffered from a lack of sufficient passing places as it was principally a single track route. It was, however, successful enough for a second route to be constructed from Junction Road to Whytescauseway via the railway station. This opened on 28 September of the same year and included a short branch to the gates at Beveridge Park. A link was installed in St Clair Street connecting the upper and lower routes. The mistakes on the Gallatown route (known as the lower route) were not repeated on the newer 'upper route', which was principally constructed as a double line. Kirkcaldy's tramway, which was municipally owned, ran on a gauge of 3 feet 6 inches and comprised a total running length of 6.5 miles using twenty-six tram cars. A substantial depot was built at Oswald Road, Gallatown, to house the tram fleet and was a prominent feature in the town until it was demolished around the 1980s. Power for the Kirkcaldy tram system was provided by a small power station constructed in Victoria Road. Construction began in 1899 and it was designed by local architect William Williamson. The first electric power was generated in December 1902, ready for the trams which would start two months later. It also provided the power for the town's street lighting and a supply for housing needs.

Another tramway system was to follow in 1906, built by Randolph Wemyss following the authorisation of the Wemyss Tramway Order of 1905. He saw the benefits of the tram system for transporting his workers between the villages and the coal pits in his ownership. The Wemyss & District Tramway Company operated 7.5 miles of track with the same 3 feet 6 inch gauge operated by its neighbour in Kirkcaldy. It was almost entirely financed by the laird himself, and for more than three-quarters of the route it was basically a ballasted sleeper-track light-railway, totally fenced in and running on private land in the grounds of Wemyss Castle. It only encroached on to the public highway for the purpose of passing along the main street of each village. The tram depot was at Aberhill, but an unusual feature was that all maintenance and overhaul of the cars was carried out by agreement by Kirkcaldy Corporation in their depot at Gallatown. A connection was made at Gallatown which allowed through running to Kirkcaldy town centre from Durie Street, Leven. A line was authorised to run from Coaltown to Dysart but was never constructed. The Wemyss Tramway Company used a total of seventeen tramcars initially, but by the end this had risen to twenty-nine throughout its operating life. Because of the 'light railway' nature of the Wemyss system, all tramcars were to a single deck layout. Even when Kirkcaldy's double deck trams eventually ran over the Wemyss metals, no passengers were allowed to travel on the upper decks. In 1912, the Balfour Beatty group took financial control of the Wemyss Tramway Company, the second feather in the cap of their Fife Tramway Light & Power Company (they already had the Dunfermline & District Tramways Company under their belt). Kirkcaldy Town Council marched on, rejecting all plans for motor bus services along their tram routes until they were challenged in 1927 and subsequently acknowledged the fact that they had no powers to do so. Thus, the same fate now befell the Kirkcaldy trams that had previously plagued the Wemyss Tramways – the over indulgence of motor buses and the bus piracy involved with it.

Kirkcaldy Corporation Tramways ceased running on 15 May 1931 when it was no longer feasible to operate against the competing bus services. The Wemyss system lasted not much longer and ceased running on 30 January 1932, although two of the Wemyss 8-wheeled, single deck cars saw further service with the Dunfermline & District Tramway Company until it too ceased running in 1937.

Motor buses didn't get a foothold in Kirkcaldy until 1913 when what was to become Fife's biggest operator, the General Motor Carrying Company, was created by a couple of brothers-in-law who ran a haulage business. They ran their business during the week for J. & J. Todd, a flour milling company, but at the weekends changed the lorry bodies for charabanc bodies to get full use of the vehicles. They started running in the summer of that year from Kirkcaldy to Burntisland via Kinghorn. Due to the success of this venture, further routes were soon to follow. It was also at this time that they purchased their first buses for these new routes. Eventually the GMC Company became the biggest operators in the area, having a virtual monopoly of services around Kirkcaldy.

After the war, there was an explosion of operators running services around Kirkcaldy, due mainly to the availability of surplus vehicles and chassis from the military. The town centre was free of these operators as the Town Council banned buses from operating within the burgh boundary, to protect their tramway system from competition. The various operators in the area operated their own routes; many prospered if they were ambitious enough, while others fell by the wayside through lack of ambition. Due to this increased competition from the motor bus companies along the tram routes, and the bus 'piracy' introduced as mentioned earlier, the Wemyss Tramway Company introduced their own buses from July 1922, to compete with the other operators along the route. The tram depot at Aberhill had a bus garage added to the site to house the new bus side of operations. Initially, the tramway company buses ran parallel to the tramway route, to try and drive off the other operators' vehicles or 'chasers'. The Wemyss Tramway bus department soon began a policy of acquiring the smaller independent operators and eventually, in 1926, gained the controlling interest in the General Motor Carrying Company of Kirkcaldy. It continued to operate independently, but was done so as a more co-ordinated operation because of the Wemyss Company shareholding.

In April 1931, Balfour Beatty, which was the controlling interest in the Fife Tramway Light & Power Company, of which Wemyss Tramways was a subsidiary, passed control of all their bus subsidiaries to Walter Alexander. All assets and vehicles were passed to the local operations company (GMC) while the Wemyss Company was wound up in 1938. To quote a well-used cliché, the rest, as they say, is history.

The various liveries used by the main operators mentioned in this book were as follows. Kirkcaldy Corporation Tramways used a livery of dark bronze, green and cream. The Wemyss & District Tramway Company used two liveries. The first was called 'Wemyss Yellow' which gave rise to the tramcar nicknames of 'mustard boxes'. The livery later changed to maroon and yellow. The Wemyss Tramways buses were painted in a dark red and cream livery, while vehicles used by the General Motor Carrying Company were painted in a rather bland slate grey. Around 1930, some of their vehicles received a red and cream livery, but from about 1932 they were being repainted into Alexander's blue livery. For the next 30 years this livery remained unchanged, until 1962, when a year after the Alexander's empire split into three operating areas, Fife vehicles began to emerge in the familiar Ayres red and cream.

Between 1962 and 1991, Fife's vehicles remained in the much loved red and cream livery. The same colours remained even when the company, by this time known as Fife Scottish, started in the mid-1980s to adopt the 'large logo' scheme, which was basically more cream and less red. It all changed again from 1991 when Stagecoach bought the Fife Scottish company after the introduction of privatisation. Stagecoach started to repaint the buses in their own 'stripy' or 'candy stripe' livery. Stagecoach changed their identity once more around 2002, and it is this 'swirl' livery that is still around on the buses operated by Stagecoach in Fife at present.

The services in central Fife have adapted to the increase in needs of the various communities; indeed, the area has a marvellous network of services connecting local communities with the various hospitals, schools, industries and town centres around the region. A lot of these services have continued due to the working relationship Stagecoach have with Fife Council.

Bus depots used at present by companies running services can be found at Aberhill and Glenrothes. Moffat & Williamson also have a depot within Glenrothes. At present, Kirkcaldy, the principal town in the area, has no depot for bus operations, although there are rumours circulating suggesting that things may change in the future.

When the original Kirkcaldy Esplanade depot closed in 2004, the Fife company headquarters moved, albeit temporarily, to premises at Glenfield Industrial Estate in Cowdenbeath. It would later move back to Kirkcaldy in 2009, to new purpose-built premises in the John Smith Business Park to the north of the town. This is now the head office for Stagecoach East Scotland.

No matter what changes happen to bus liveries, or who operates whatever service with whatever type of bus, Kirkcaldy and central Fife will continue to enjoy the comprehensive network of services it has had since it all started over a hundred years ago with the horse and carriage. In a way, we have travelled full circle, as we started off with one kind of stage coach, and finish with the Stagecoach we have at present. Bon Voyage!

Before the advent of the tramway system, this is how Kirkcaldy citizens used to travel. This early image shows the town's High Street in 1824 with a fully laden stage coach, no doubt departing for one of the other towns in the county. (*Bill Dewar*)

We are now 79 years further on, and we see here the opening ceremonies of the Kirkcaldy Corporation Tramways system in 1903. This was taken near the workshops at the terminus at Gallatown, before the guests headed back to the town centre in the decorated tramcars.

The proud staff at Gallatown, Kirkcaldy, are seen posing for a photograph outside the newly completed tram depot in 1903. The former tram depot was demolished in the 1980s after having been used as a works by Walter Alexander's bus company and by a local merchant, Thomas Muir.

Another photograph of the staff at Gallatown, this time showing a full house inside the car shed. It looks very claustrophobic compared to the Wemyss car shed at Aberhill, possibly due to the closeness of the running lines and the many maintenance pits.

More of a posed image here, as the staff line up beside each of the tramcars on show. Included among the staff are the various tradesmen, motormen and conductors employed by the tramcar company. This must have still been the early days as the workshop floor looks pretty clean and everything looks neat and tidy. (*Bill Dewar*)

Here we see car number 13 at the terminus at Gallatown in the area near the former Turret bar. From Gallatown, the line ran to the terminus at Linktown via the path and the High Street. A junction was also laid at the bottom of St Clair Street for trams heading to Dysart, and a junction was placed at the aptly named Junction Road for services to Whytescauseway via the 'upper route'.

Dysart is the location, as we see another old picture postcard scene of a tram about to head up Normand Road from Townhead. The terminus in Dysart was at the top of the hill, at a loop adjacent to Fraser Place. It will be noticed that a lot of old postcards were 'colourised' at the beginning of the twentieth century to add appeal when no colour film was available.

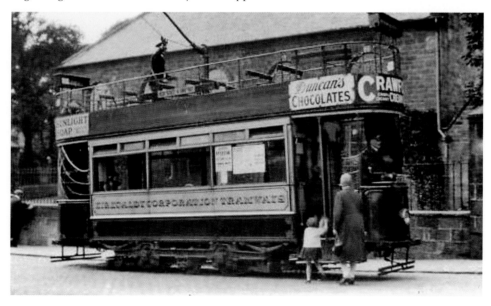

The same location at Townhead in Dysart, but looking in the direction of the Barony Church in the background. A mother and daughter are seen boarding the tramcar for the short trip up Normand Road to the terminus.

Another colourised picture postcard shows one of the tramcars on one of the passing loops along Link Street. The various representations of the tramcar livery were a bit vague, and many variations will be seen in these early pages.

Tramcar number 19 is seen here sitting at the terminus at the west end of Link Street, Kirkcaldy. None of the buildings seen here remain, and the area is now unrecognisable from this image.

A wider view of the same area at the Link Street terminus. Apart from the building on the extreme right (the former Starks bar), nothing else remains. The tenements seen near the bottom of Pratt Street have been replaced by more modern flats. The Commer vehicle, S7882, is seen dropping off passengers on a General Motor Carrying Company service from Burntisland. This dates the image as being after 1913.

A fine image shows tramcar number 9 at the terminus at the bottom of Whytescauseway. The junction here led to either, on the left, the terminus at Linktown, or back along the High Street on the right.

This picture post card image shows car number 6 passing the bottom of Whytescauseway. This image can be dated to being before November 1903 as the junction from the upper route has not been installed yet.

This view of the same area as seen in the previous image clearly shows the junction now in place at the bottom of Whytescauseway. Although taken more than a century ago, this area still looks very much identifiable when passing from the west today.

Although no trams or buses are on show, this photograph is included to show the area along Victoria Road where the main industry was the manufacture of linoleum. It appears to be the end of a shift, as a lot of the employees can be seen leaving the factory. The tram lines and overhead power lines can clearly be seen in the image. (*Bill Dewar*)

Tramcar 16 is seen near the park gates on Abbotshall Road in Kirkcaldy. This short section of track branched off the main route to Whytescauseway at a junction at the bottom of Bennochy Road and terminated at the entrance to Beverage Park.

This is a general view taken at the west end of Kirkcaldy High Street and looking back to the east. The road here is quite wide and tramcar number 8 poses no problem to the other road users as it makes its way to the terminus at Linktown.

Another view of Kirkcaldy High Street, taken near Kirk Wynd in the later half of the 1920s. The dress wear doesn't look as formal as in the earlier images, and what appears to be either some kind of motorised bicycle, or a tricycle and basket, can be seen on the right hand side of the photograph.

The local bare-footed street urchins pay no attention as tramcar number 4 passes by, trundling down through the High Street toward the east end and beyond. You may have noticed that most people, including everyone in this photograph, wore a cap or a hat of some description in the early part of the twentieth century.

Another view taken at the west end of the High Street, looking eastwards towards the junction further back along the road at Whytescauseway. This is the area at the junction with Nicol Street and Links Street.

Tramcar 11 is seen passing an area at the east end of Kirkcaldy High Street known as the 'Sailors Walk'. I am unsure of the origin for the name, but it is in close proximity to the harbour. Beyond this image, the route takes us up The Path and subsequently to Gallatown.

In this view we can see the rather scant appearance of the inside of the tram depot at Aberhill. This appearance is deceptive, I believe due to the Aberhill depot only having one open pit and more room between tracks compared to the photograph of the inside of the depot at Gallatown.

A fine view here of tramcar number 18 taken at Aberhill. The car was manufactured by Brush Electrical Engineering at their Falcon Works in Loughborough and is pictured not long after arriving in Methil in January 1925. This tramcar, along with its sister, number 19, was bought by the Dunfermline Tramways company in 1932 and saw another 5 years' service in west Fife.

This was the eastern extent of the Wemyss & District Tramways system. It is the terminus at Carberry Gates, with Scoonie Road disappearing into the distance. Tramcar number 10 sits for a few minutes before heading back towards Kirkcaldy. (*Bill Dewar*)

Shorehead is the location for this image as we see tramcar number 9 making steady progress through the streets. The tramcars always seemed to attract the crowds, especially young kids, some of whom can be seen here bare-footed, and some who had families wealthy enough to provide shoes.

Wemyss tramcar number 2 is seen travelling through Leven High Street on opening day, 25 August 1906. It is being ably assisted by some of the local bare-footed youths, who no doubt found the whole experience to still be a bit of a novelty. (*Bill Dewar*)

A fine image showing tramcar number 15 at the terminus in Durie Street, Leven. The driver and conductor look almost military in their appearance, which was practically normal in those days.

Tramcar number 9 was one of the original four-wheeled tramcars built by the Brush Traction Company at their Falcon works in Loughborough and is seen outside the depot at Aberhill. Like their Kirkcaldy counterparts, the driver and conductor are almost military in their appearance.

Tramcar number 28 was one of the eight tramcars inherited from the Kirkcaldy Company in 1931. It ran for less than a year before it was withdrawn alongside the rest of the Wemyss tramcar fleet in January 1932.

Tramcar number 6 is seen here in Bridge Street in Leven. The track in this area was initially single, but was doubled in 1914. It was common for postcard publishers to edit out the smoke from the local chimneys and add a cloud or two when they were colourising the cards.

21

Main St. Coaltown

Another colourised old picture postcard sees one of the Wemyss tramcars running along the Main Street through Coaltown of Wemyss. The line, when later doubled, was diverted to run along the back of the Main Street.

One of the Kirkcaldy tramcars, on hire to the Wemyss Company, is seen trundling eastwards through the Wemyss estate on the reserved track, having just passed the north lodge gates. This area is at the small roundabout at the top of Boreland Road in Kirkcaldy. (*Bill Dewar*)

The Rosie Pit Cottages.

Wemyss tramcar number 10 is seen passing the Rosie Pit cottages at Wellsgreen, to the north of Macduff Castle. The Rosie Pit was located somewhere off to the right of the photograph.

Wemyss & District Tramway. DENBEATH.

Denbeath is the location of this image showing one of the tramcars heading east, bound for Leven. Denbeath Bridge would not be too far from this location as it is assumed that the building on the right is a part of the Wellesley Pit complex. (*Bill Dewar*)

Tramcar number 4 is pictured here outside the original three-road depot at Aberhill. The depot would eventually be enhanced by a further three-road shed added on, as well as an outside holding siding. The Wemyss tower wagon can be seen alongside car 4. (*Bill Dewar*)

This colourised image shows one of the Wemyss tramcars at the Gallatown terminus at the junction of Randolph Road and Rosslyn Street in 1909. Even though it is merely a colourised image, you could understand why the Wemyss tramcars were nicknamed 'mustard boxes'.

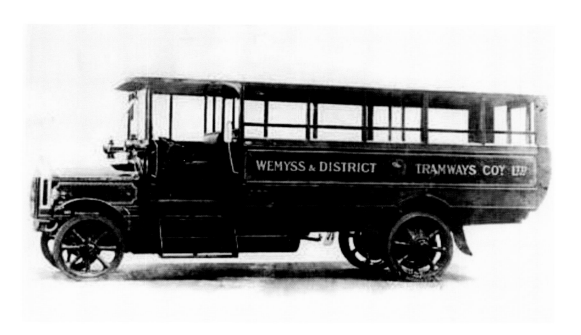

In what appears to be a posed manufacturer's photograph, we see one of the Tilling-Stevens buses purchased by the Wemyss tramways bus department to help combat the 'poaching' of passengers by the many independent operators working in the area. (*Bill Dewar*)

One of the buses operated by Walter Alexander's on the services which replaced the trams in 1931 was this Cowieson-bodied Albion, FG1939 (196). It is seen displaying a couple of paper window stickers for Gallatown and the High Street, pre-dating a common practice of the Scottish Bus Group by nearly 50 years. (*Bill Dewar*)

The driver and conductress pose in front of ex-Wemyss Tramways Albion FG1938, showing the fleet number D70 when operated by the GMC Company of Kirkcaldy. The GMC acquired several vehicles in 1932 from the Wemyss Company. (*Bill Dewar*)

A fine example of a 'Bundy Clock' seen on the wall of a house in St Clair Street, Kirkcaldy. Bundy clocks were used by tram and bus companies to ensure that vehicles did not depart early from outlying areas. (*Terry Gilley*)

Here we see the frontage of the former tram depot at Gallatown, taken sometime around the late 1960s. When the depot stopped being used by the tram company, it was taken over and run as a workshop for a while by Walter Alexander's bus company. It was, later still, used by local scrap merchant Thomas Muir before being demolished around the 1980s. (*Bill Dewar*)

This is a recent photograph of Kirkcaldy Esplanade showing, in front, the old head office, with the old paint shops behind. The head office moved from here in about 2004 and was located temporarily at an industrial estate at Cowdenbeath. It has now re-located back to Kirkcaldy, but is now at the John Smith Business Park to the north of the town.

WG3260 was an Alexander's-bodied Leyland LT5A from the 1935 intake and initially carried the fleet number N230. This was one of a batch of vehicles that were re-engined and subsequently re-numbered in 1945, ending up as P705. This bus, seen here leaving Kirkcaldy on a run to Leven, was withdrawn in 1959 but saw further use with Williamson of Gauldry until 1963, when it was sold and used as a caravan until 1979. (*John Sinclair*)

Seen at an unknown location, but with 'East Wemyss' as its destination, we find Alexander's-bodied Leyland TS7 WG6414 (P425). New in 1937 with seating for thirty-two, it was re-seated to thirty-four in June 1958 and was transferred for use on Kirkcaldy town services after being repainted in the red town service livery. It was withdrawn two years later (1960) and sold to Cullis of Glasgow. (*John Sinclair*)

AMS318 (RO543) was a 1945-built Guy Arab 2 with bodywork by Weymann. It is seen passing in front of the Esplanade bus stance in Kirkcaldy shortly before its withdrawal late in 1962. It was sold to Horne, a dealer from Denny, in February the following year. (*John Sinclair*)

AMS182 (RO492) was a Northern Counties-bodied Guy Arab 2, and is also pictured within the confines of Kirkcaldy's Esplanade depot. This bus is showing another method of displaying side panel adverts, which have been done on an independent panel and secured to the side of the bus by screws. (*Paul Redmond*)

WG3498 (P314) was an Alexander's-bodied Leyland TS7 of Walter Alexander's Aberhill depot, and is seen here while on a private hire. This bus was new to Alexander's in 1936 and lasted until 1955, when it was withdrawn from service. (*Dr George Fairbairn*)

Here we see a Guy Arab 3, AWG391 (RO605), one of the Craven's-bodied buses, sitting against the sea wall at Kirkcaldy depot in the later half of 1961. This view clearly shows the skill that was achieved by the painters in the paint shop, as side panel adverts were hand painted. This bus lasted with Fife until it was withdrawn in 1970, having served the company for 22 years. (*Paul Redmond*)

Aberhill depot is the setting for this lovely photograph of a Burlingham-bodied Leyland PS1, CWG343 (PA216). This photograph was taken before the 1961 split as the 'F' prefix has not been applied as yet. It was withdrawn in 1965 and sold to Muir's. It was then bought by a private owner at St David's Harbour (presumably Dalgety Bay) and was still there in a derelict state about twelve years later. (*John Sinclair*)

Duple-bodied single deck Guy Arab AMS559 (G29) is caught at rest between turns on the local Kirkcaldy town service no. 5 between the bus station and Dysart to the east. It should be noted that buses were always smartly turned out in the days of Walter Alexander's. (*Paul Redmond*)

A fine rear view of Craven's-bodied Guy Arab CST5 (FRO574). There is a front view of this scene in the *Fife Buses* book, also by Amberley Publishing. Across the road can be seen the entrance to Kirkcaldy's 'Ballroom'. It will be noticed that the rear fleet number is applied by hand in gold coloured lettering, which was a bit harder to make out against the red livery than the later white lettering. (*John Sinclair*)

AMS229 (RO514) is another double deck Guy Arab 2 of 1944 vintage with bodywork by Northern Counties. This vehicle lasted in the fleet until withdrawal in 1963, when it was sent to Muir's scrap yard. (*Paul Redmond*)

A group of Kirkcaldy-based conductresses are pictured here in the 1950s wearing a great selection of paraphernalia that would make a modern day collector green with envy. On show are cap badges, licence badges, various ticket machines and tickets, among other items.

Seen here parked up at a location unknown to the author, we find Aberhill depot's DWG525 (FPC29). This vehicle was a Leyland PSU1/15 with Leyland's own bodywork. It carries the Alexander's coach livery as applied after 1962, and although not seen here, had a central door, which in 1965 was repositioned nearer to the front of this vehicle. It was withdrawn from the Fife fleet in 1970 and sold to a dealer in Preston. (*John Sinclair*)

Here is an image of the sister vehicle of that seen in the previous photograph. This one is DWG692 (FPC35) and is seen parked up on Kirkcaldy promenade wearing the new Fife colours as originally applied after 1962. (*John Sinclair*)

Guy Arab AMS232 (FRO517) is seen wearing its newly applied Fife livery of Ayres red and cream while taking a rest at Kirkcaldy bus station. Further embellishments include the screwed on blank side advert panel and the painted on 'town service' headboard. It is on local service 11 to Glamis Road within the town. (*Paul Redmond*)

A beautiful photograph showing a quartet of Guy Arab buses sitting at the layover area in Kirkcaldy's town bus station. This image can be dated to 1962 as that was the year the Fife area buses were painted Ayres red, and the year in which Northern Counties-bodied Guy Arab 2 AMS183 (RO493) received the 'F' prefix in the fleet number, which it has not received in this image. (*John Sinclair*)

Kirkcaldy-based Guy Arab AMS236 (RO521) with Northern Counties bodywork is seen here during the 1961–62 transitional period. It has just pulled into the town's bus station on a local service no. 7 from Smeaton to the town centre. (*Paul Redmond*)

By the time this photograph of WG8118 (FP539) was taken in July 1962, it was twenty-three years old, making it one of the oldest vehicles in the Fife fleet at the time. It was a Leyland TS8 with Alexander's bodywork and was new in 1939. It is a Lochgelly depot vehicle but is seen leaving the workshops in Kirkcaldy. It was also painted in coach livery for work on the Queensferry Passage Ferry. (*John Sinclair*)

Glasgow is the location here of Aberhill's AWG550 (FPA15), a Leyland Tiger PS1 dating from 1947 with Alexander's own bodywork. It will soon be heading back on the arduous journey to Leven on service no. 27. (*Paul Redmond*)

The distinct lines of BMS593 (FG71), a Kirkcaldy-based Guy Arab 3 with Massey bodywork dating from 1948, can be clearly seen in this view taken at the layover area at the town bus station. (*Paul Redmond*)

AWG574 (FG60) was a Guy Arab 3 with Brockhouse bodywork and was one of Alexander's 1948 in-take of vehicles. It is seen here having been withdrawn due to accident damage at Kirkcaldy depot in April 1965; it made it into the Fife fleet at the 1961 split and gained the Ayres red livery and 'F' prefix. The following month would see it at Muir's scrapyard on the other side of Kirkcaldy. (*John Sinclair*)

Albion Victor FT3AB, CWG228 (FBA3), looks somewhat squeezed in beside some of its stable mates in this shot taken inside the main shed on the Esplanade, Kirkcaldy. This was one of five ordered in 1950 with Strachan bodywork; they were somewhat unique in being petrol engined vehicles. This vehicle ended up in Muir's scrapyard in 1964. (*Paul Redmond*)

The central vehicle, GYL450 (RO704), is a 1946 Guy Arab 2 with bodywork by Northern Counties. It was new to London Transport but acquired by Alexander's in 1953. The two outer vehicles are Guy Arab 3s with the curvier Craven's bodywork. AWG393 (FRO607) and AWG380 (RO594) were new to Walter Alexander's in 1948. All eventually ended up at Muir's scrapyard although FRO607 ended up preserved. (*John Sinclair*)

Leyland PS1, DMS816 (FPB3) with Alexander's bodywork is seen sitting at the front of Kirkcaldy bus depot in coach livery. It was initially an OPS2/1 model when new in 1951, but was converted in 1960 by the transfer of parts from other withdrawn PS1s. It was withdrawn itself in 1970 and was last reported as part of a contract fleet in Weaverham, Cheshire. (*Paul Redmond*)

Bristol FS6B Lodekka BXA457B (FRD192) travels up Bennochy Road from Kirkcaldy bus station during May 1978, and is making steady progress towards its destination. The service no. 8 travelled via Bennochy Bridge, Strathkinnes Road and Brodick Road before reaching Glamis Road to the north of the town. (*Stephen Dowle*)

Alexander's-bodied Leyland PSU1/15 EMS170 (PC52) of Dunfermline depot is seen here parked up near the sea wall at Kirkcaldy depot in 1962. It has just come from the paint shop across the road and would soon receive the 'F' prefix to the fleet number. This bus was rebuilt with a forward entrance door in 1965. It was withdraw five years later in 1970 and sold to a dealer in Preston. (*Paul Redmond*)

Seen at the back of the yard in Kirkcaldy depot, having been stripped of a few parts following accident damage and subsequent withdrawal, we see Eastern Coach Works-bodied Leyland PD1 CCS407 (FRB163) sitting alongside Alexander's-bodied Leyland PS1 BWG510 (FPA105). Both vehicles were scrapped in 1970 up the road at Muir's scrapyard. FRB163 was an acquisition from Western SMT in 1967, although it had been on loan since 1966. (*John Sinclair*)

FWG845 (E10) was one of twenty Bristol LS6G buses bought by Walter Alexander's in 1955 with Eastern Coach Works bodywork. They all served their time in Fife until they were withdrawn in the mid-1970s. E10 is another bus just repainted into the new Ayres red livery in 1962 and is also waiting its 'F' prefix to be added to the fleet number. (*Paul Redmond*)

Here we see another of the LS6G buses based in Kirkcaldy. This one, FWG854 (FE19), is seen in the second half of the 1960s and in my opinion is further enhanced by the application of cream paint around the windows as well as the waist. This vehicle was scrapped and salvaged for re-useable parts by Alexander's (Fife) in 1975. (*Barry Sanjana*)

Seen photographed against the depot wall in Kirkcaldy, we see the four Albion Lowlander buses that came from Western SMT in April 1966. A further five would arrive by the end of December that year. They are still in the livery of their previous owner, and still carry their old fleet numbers. From the left, they would eventually become FRE27, 26, 29 and 28 in the Fife fleet. (*John Sinclair*)

Another FLF Lodekka in the shape of Kirkcaldy based HXA408E (FRD208). It is seen at rest on the main road on the Esplanade, having just arrived from Glenrothes on service 394. It was normal practice for buses to use the seafront road for laying over as the bus station offered limited space for this purpose. Remember, roads were a lot quieter in those days. (*Grahame Wareham*)

This FS Lodekka, JWG92 (FRD37), was one of the buses fitted with brackets to allow the placing of the 'town services' headboard when used for that purpose in Kirkcaldy. It is seen displaying one of the typical side advertisements of the era, for Haig Whisky. (*Innes Cameron*)

Another vehicle parked up within the limited confines of the seafront bus station is this 1957 Alexander's-bodied Guy Arab LUF, JWG503 (FGA12). It is a Kirkcaldy depot vehicle and is being used on a short run up the coast to East Wemyss. This vehicle was withdrawn in 1972. (*Barry Sanjana*)

BMS863 (G83) was a Guy Arab 3 with bodywork by the same manufacturer (Guy). It is pictured in Kirkcaldy town bus station in between runs on local service no. 7 to and from Smeaton. It was new in March 1948 and lasted eighteen years in the Kingdom, finally being withdrawn in 1966. It ended up at Muir's scrapyard in March 1967. (*John Sinclair*)

Leyland PSU1/15 DWG694 (FPC37) rests at the rear of Aberhill depot sometime in the second half of the 1960s. It was new in 1952 and was built with the door in the centre of the body. When it was rebuilt in 1966, the entrance door was moved to the front of the vehicle. It was withdrawn in 1970 and sold for scrap the following year to Muir's. (*John Sinclair*)

Bedford VAS1 BXA608B (FW5) is seen parked up at Killermont, Glasgow, having not long arrived on a run from Kirkcaldy. It was new in 1964 and was bodied by Duple to a coach specification, and was both light in weight and bright inside. It was withdrawn in 1972 and went through a couple of dealers before seeing further use with Richards Brothers of Moylgrove. (*John Sinclair*)

A Northern Counties-bodied Albion Lowlander, UCS613 (FRE35), is shown here in Kirkcaldy depot displaying its plainness for all to see. Acquired from Western SMT in 1967, it was a rather unremarkable looking vehicle, but still an improvement on Alexander's own interpretation of the bodywork for this chassis. (*Innes Cameron*)

Something old, something new... Here we see one of the oldest vehicles in the fleet, Guy Arab 2 AMS211 (T1) of 1945 vintage beside Alexander's-bodied Daimler Fleetline LXA406G (FRF6) which, when pictured in October 1969, was only a year old. AMS211 was retired in 1971 and ended up preserved in Burton. The Fife area head office can be seen across the road. (*John Sinclair*)

Another one of Kirkcaldy depot's long serving workhorses is seen parked up against the sea wall at the rear of the depot yard. MMS733 (FRD81) was new to the Walter Alexander's company in 1959 and served its entire life in Fife at Kirkcaldy depot. This was an LD6G model and was withdrawn in 1975, ending up at the (in)famous Muir's scrapyard. (*Barry Sanjana*)

A fine image of Alexander's-bodied Albion Viking MXA637G (FNV37), seen here at Kirkcaldy bus station sometime near the end of the 1980s. It almost looks brand new and has obviously just had a new paint job as it readies to depart on service no. 5 up the coast to Bonnybank. (*Steven Dowle*)

A rear image shot of the vehicle in the previous photograph. It is included here to illustrate the rear end arrangement of the grilles for the Alexander's-bodied Viking as this type of vehicle had a centrally mounted, longitudinal engine. (*Steven Dowle*)

It is August 1968 and we see the arrival of LXA404G (FRF4) at Kirkcaldy bus depot. It has just come from Alexander's factory in Falkirk and made the journey on trade plates. Other members of staff can be seen looking on at the new arrivals, perhaps with a little trepidation. (*John Sinclair*)

Also delivered to Fife in 1971, and based in Kirkcaldy, was this Eastern Coach Works-bodied Daimler Fleetline PXA636J (FRF36). It too is seen at the Esplanade bus station and will be heading for Leslie via Glenrothes on service 339. The ECW bodies came with white/cream window rubbers which enhanced, and complimented, the cream relief of the bus livery. (*Grahame Wareham*)

1967 saw the arrival of the last of the new Lodekkas when eighteen FLF6G models arrived. HXA408E (FRD208) is one of this batch and is seen sitting near Kirkcaldy Esplanade, waiting time for its next journey to Lochgelly on service 334 via Bowhill. This service left the Esplanade bus station on the hour and the half hour and had a journey time of 35 minutes. (*Robert Dickson*)

Here is Daimler Fleetline LXA403G (FRF3) with the original style of lower front panel. I think the Alexander's styling for the Fleetline was the best looking on the market. This photograph also shows the original style of cream relief with black lining. (*Grahame Wareham*)

A rather clean looking Alexander's-bodied Daimler Fleetline, RXA50J (FRF50), is seen sitting patiently at the Esplanade bus stance in Kirkcaldy in August 1972. It was on service 394 to Glenrothes (Glenwood) via Gallatown, Thornton and Glenrothes town centre. (*Grahame Wareham*)

Bristol FLF Lodekka HXA412E (FRD212) is captured in Bennochy Road, Kirkcaldy, dropping off passengers near the Adam Smith Centre on service 339. It had originated in Leslie and had travelled via Glenrothes, Thornton and Gallatown before terminating at the Esplanade bus stance. (*Claire Pendrous*)

Alexander's-bodied AEC Reliance 7425SP (FAC5) is barely two months old when seen parked outside the Gallatown workshops on 4 July 1962. The workshop at Gallatown was the old tram depot and is easily recognisable by its architecture. The rear view of this bus shows the flowing curves carried by this particular body style. (*John Sinclair*)

Another Lodekka, but of the FS6G model, is pictured on a local school run in Glenrothes. 3657FG (FRD171) has just left Auchmuty High School with the rear doors closed for the kids' own safety, and is seen sporting a smart wrap-around advert for a local Volkswagen car dealer in the area. (*John Law*)

One of the Alexander's-bodied Albion Lowlanders, UCS623 (FRE38), a vehicle acquired from Western SMT in 1967, is seen sitting in the yard at Kirkcaldy depot sporting another variation of the livery as applied to this vehicle type. (*Innes Cameron*)

This Alexander's Y-type Ford R1114, HSF557N (FT12), was only six months old when seen on 13 August 1975, leaving the Esplanade bus station in Kirkcaldy bound for Glenrothes. All seven of the Alexander's-bodied Ford buses were transferred to Highland Omnibuses in 1982. (*John Sinclair*)

The Bristol RELL did sterling work for Alexander's (Fife) in the Kirkcaldy area. JXA923F (FE23) is shown here plying its trade on a local service between the Esplanade and Chapel West to the north-west of the town. FE23 is shown here with the lowered cream waist band as applied when the fleet name changed to the Fife Scottish logo. (*Paul Redmond*)

Bristol FLF6G Lodekka HXA408E (FRD208) is seen here heading down the coast for Burntisland. The location and date are unknown to me, but I do know there were two or three short working to Colinswell in Burntisland from Gallatown, principally for the use of factory workers, so the location will probably be somewhere in Kirkcaldy.

FS6G type Lodekka 3660FG (FRD174) is seen parked up at the layover area in Kirkcaldy bus station in April 1979. It has obviously been on a route of some description, but must be near the end of its time with the Fife company as there are number blinds missing and the fleet name has been removed. (*Robert Dickson*)

Bristol RELL JXA922F (FE22) is captured here entering the yard at Kirkcaldy depot. Twelve of these vehicles arrived in Fife in 1968 and worked on inter urban services in the Kingdom. Fife was the only SBG subsidiary to order and operate the Bristol RELL. (*Robert Dickson*)

This Aberhill-based Duple-bodied Ford R1014, HSF552N (FT7), was also six months old when photographed in Arbroath on 31 July 1975. This vehicle carries coach bodywork by Duple and seated forty-five passengers. This vehicle, and four others in the batch, were sold on to Alexander's (Northern) in 1979. (*John Sinclair*)

Kirkcaldy, like the other Fife depots, needed to train drivers and 3664FG, formerly Bristol FLF6G Lodekka with fleet number FRD178, fitted the bill when it was withdrawn. Many withdrawn vehicles were used by the Fife bus company throughout the years. (*Clive A. Brown*)

Mk 1 Ailsa LSX28P (FRA28) passes the 'Ex Terra' statue outside the entrance to Glenrothes bus station as it travels to its final destination in one of the local areas in the new town. The conductress can be seen standing at the front of the bus with the sleeves rolled up. It must have been a busy shift.

This Kirkcaldy-based Albion Viking, FXA725D (FNV25), is seen on a beautiful day on 16 April 1967 at the Esplanade bus stance as it readies itself for a journey to Perth via Cowdenbeath, Kelty and Glenfarg. This was one of thirteen delivered in 1966 with the bodies completed by Potter of Belfast, an Alexander's subsidiary company. (*John Sinclair*)

Bristol FLF6G Lodekka HXA405E (FRD205) turns from the west end of Kirkcaldy High Street down towards the Esplanade bus station on a service no. 6 from Dunfermline to Upper Largo. This service travelled via Donibristle Estate and Lower Methil, as opposed to the no. 7 which ran via Dalgety Bay and Aberhill. (*Robert Dickson*)

LD6G Lodekka RWG374 (ex FRD151) is seen passing the swimming pool and heading west along Kirkcaldy promenade after having a trip out and about, around Fife, with a group of new hopeful drivers. (*Dr George Fairbairn*)

This Alexander's M-type Leyland Leopard, HSX64N (FPE64), is makng steady progress between Glenrothes and Kirkcaldy on 31 July 1978. It was only four months old at the time of this photograph and had probably racked up the miles already. This initial livery was a version of the Ayres red and cream colours applied to coaches at the time. (*John Sinclair*)

Another view of FPE64 taken at the Esplanade bus stance on the same day as the previous photograph. This livery wouldn't last much longer as Fife fell into line with the other Scottish Bus Group companies and adopted a blue and white colour scheme for express services to London. (*John Sinclair*)

And here it is. The same coach as in the previous picture, FPE64, but now wearing the livery that was to become synonymous with long distance work between Scotland and London and was the predecessor to the well known Citylink network. Note the Fife script-style fleet name below the windscreen.

Again, FPE64 is seen within the yard at Kirkcaldy depot, sitting beside sister vehicle HSX65N (FPE65). They are just biding their time before their next overnight journey to London. The fleet name below the window is now of the corporate style.

Hiding away in the shed at Kirkcaldy depot, we this find Alexander's Y-type-bodied Bristol RE, EWS169D (FE34), on 17 July 1978. Due to the nature of the long-distance runs done by these vehicles, they were principally nocturnal beasts, although they were often spotted during the day on runs between Fife and Glasgow. (*John Sinclair*)

A fine line-up of Guy Arab 3 single-deckers is seen sitting in Muir's scrapyard in Kirkcaldy in the late 1960s. There are bodies by four different manufacturers on show (Duple, Brockhouse, Guy and Massey) and, given the chance, all these buses look like they would start at the first attempt. (*John Sinclair*)

More buses seen in Muir's scrapyard, including one of many Eastern Scottish vehicles that also found their way across the Forth to meet their fate. It is in the company of a handful of Fife's double deckers including Lodekka 7406SP (FRD158). (*Robert Dickson*)

A18AXA (L5) was one of Fife's former Lodekkas and was converted into a tow wagon in July 1972. It was formerly GWG984 (FRD8) and is seen here manoeuvring into the yard at Kirkcaldy depot with one of Fife's coach liveried Y-types in tow. (*Stephen Dowle*)

One of the original twenty Alexander's-bodied Daimler Fleetlines, new in 1968, is seen here turning up Whytescauseway en route to Kirkcaldy bus station. LXA412G (FRF12) is seen with the original style front panel which at the time (1968) was the most stylish when compared to that offered by the other manufacturers at the time. (*Paul Redmond*)

WFS139W (PE139) was one of the 1980 batch of Alexander's Y-type Leyland Leopards delivered without the 'F' prefix letter in the fleet number. It is seen here on the no. 57 service to Edinburgh via Kinghorn, Burntisland and Aberdour. There was anger when this service was cancelled years ago but it has recently been re-introduced by Stagecoach Fife, although it is now curtailed at Ferrytoll, where a connection can be made for Edinburgh. (*Robert Dickson*)

Parked up at Leven bus station in October 1986, we find Mk 2 Ailsa OSC62V (FRA62) at rest in the layover area having done a school run that morning to St Andrews High School. This is not a school in St Andrews but a Roman Catholic high school in Kirkcaldy. (*Robert Dickson*)

In this photograph from May 1988, we see Alexander's P-type Leyland Tiger D713CSC (413), of Cowdenbeath depot, leaving Kirkcaldy bus station on a service 33 to Ballingry. This run took in Chapel Village, Cluny, Cardenden and Lochgelly. These P-type buses were affectionately known as 'portacabins' because of their square shape. (*Robert Dickson*)

Alexander's Y-type Leyland Leopard PSX184Y (184) was one of the final batch of ten new Y-types delivered in 1982. They were unique in having no overhead luggage racks and were delivered without the 'F' prefix in the fleet number. It is seen entering Kirkcaldy bus station during May 1988 on a service 39 from Leslie via Glenrothes. (*Robert Dickson*)

The main competition for Fife Scottish in Central Fife came from Moffat & Williamson, based in Gauldry; they also had depots in Gauldry and Glenrothes, the latter being where Alexander's Leyland Atlantean YBK336V was based. This bus was new in 1979 to the City of Portsmouth as their fleet number 336, but is seen here leaving Glenrothes bus station on a local service in 1993. (*John Law*)

One of the Alexander's Y-type Leyland Leopards in the Moffat & Williamson fleet, GMS294S, is seen here at their depot in Glenrothes. This was an ex-Midland Scottish vehicle and carried their fleet number MPE294. Moffat & Williamson removed the stepped aluminium waistband strips and added a black plastic strip lower down the body – an improvement to some, sacrilege to others. (*Kenneth Barclay*)

Not exactly the best looking Bristol VRT in the world. GOG630N was new to West Midlands PTE in 1974 as their fleet number 4630. It was also based in Glenrothes and is seen here at rest in the layover area at Glenrothes bus station in March 1992. (*John Law*)

Bristol VRT PJO445P is more what you would expect a VRT to look like. This example, acquired around 1987, was new to the City of Oxford as their fleet number 445 in 1975. It is seen here entering Kirkcaldy bus station in May 1991. (*John Law*)

F60RFS (60) was one of twenty MCW Metrorider minibuses ordered by Fife Scottish in 1988, a time when the Scottish Bus Group went minibus crazy in preparation for the impending privatisation of the industry. These MCW minibuses plied their trade around Kirkcaldy, working on the many local town services in the area. (*Kenneth Barclay*)

Mk 2 Ailsa OSC55V (855) is seen at Kirkcaldy depot wearing an all-over advert for the local Asda superstore at Dunnikier/Gallatown. One of the Ailsa buses at Dunfermline depot was painted the same way for the Dunfermline, Halbeath superstore. (*Kenneth Barclay*)

In 1983, Fife Scottish needed additional buses for school contracts and sourced six Daimler Fleetlines, three from Grampian and three from Tayside. In the following year ten Leyland Atlanteans arrived from Grampian. These were the first Atlanteans for Fife and were numbered in a new FRN class. Seen here in September 1987 at Kirkcaldy garage is withdrawn NRG164M (FRN4). Note the fleet names painted over prior to disposal. (*Steve Vallance*)

New to Fife Scottish Omnibuses in 1979, RSG824V (FPN24) was an 11.6 metre, Mk 2 Leyland National without a roof-mounted heater pod. This one was allocated to Lochgelly depot and is seen on a well patronised run back to its home town on the no. 34 service via Chapel Village, Cluny and Cardenden. (*Robert Dickson*)

Hopefully just an exchange of pleasantries as C799USG (FRA99), an Alexander's R-type-bodied Volvo Citybus, departs for Leven on a run from the capital. 'Fife Coastliner' was the branding for vehicles used on the no. 57 service between Leven and Edinburgh via the Fife coast. (*Gordon Stirling*)

Y-type Leopard YSF100S (100) is seen here leaving Kirkcaldy bus station on a local service, no. 89A to Westwood Avenue, during the winter of 1991. It had been snowing quite heavily earlier on that day, hence the accumulation of snow around the front grille area. The large logo livery on this vehicle included the removal of the cream around the window pillars. (*Gordon Stirling*)

Kirkcaldy-based tow wagon A18AXA (L5) is seen here in the red livery as applied to tow wagons in the 1960s and early 1970s. It is a former Lodekka, GWG984 (FRD8) and an image of it in later bright orange livery can be seen in *Fife Buses*, also by Amberley Publishing. (*John Sinclair*)

Ailsa Citybus C806USG (FRA106) is seen in George Street, Edinburgh, wearing a version of the Fife livery applied to certain vehicles used on longer distance runs. This livery was used on vehicles on express runs between Fife and Glasgow for a while, but this particular bus is carrying a 'Coastliner' headboard for use on the Fife to Edinburgh service, no. 57. (*Barry Sanjana*)

Painted in the same way as the Ailsa in a previous photograph, we see Mk 1 Leyland National HSC101T (301) sporting the all over Asda advert. This was Fife's first Leyland National, new in 1978, and was an 11.3 metre long variant with roof mounted heater pod. (*Kenneth Barclay*)

Albion Viking MXA640G (FNV40) is seen in April 1981, heading towards the east end of Kirkcaldy High Street, and ultimately Dysart, on a local service no. 81 from the railway station. This service had three buses an hour and travelled via Raith Gates, High Street, and Ravenscraig Flats before terminating at Cook Street in Dysart. The return journey was different to this route as the High Street was one way. (*Robert Dickson*)

Another photograph taken at Kirkcaldy bus station in 1991 shows a couple of Ailsa buses and a couple of Leyland Leopards seemingly huddled together to keep warm. Ailsa KSF3N (803), on the right, was a recent acquisition from Highland Scottish which saw the vehicle return to its native home. (*Gordon Stirling*)

Y-type Leopard YSF98S (FPE98) is seen heading down Kirkcaldy High Street from the west en route to the bus station. It seems this was not a busy service as there are only two passengers aboard. This is one of the rare occasions where a Y-type carried a side advertisement. (*Robert Dickson*)

Seen here leaving Kirkcaldy at the rail bridge at Seafield, we find A984FLS (FRO4), one of the first batch of ten Leyland Olympian buses that arrived in Fife in 1983. They introduced Alexander's R-type bodywork to the area, but all were subsequently sold on before Stagecoach bought the Fife company in 1991.

Leyland Leopard WFS144W (PE144) was one of the batch of buses which arrived in Fife in 1980 without the 'F' prefix letter in the fleet number. It was during this era that Fife experimented with wide cream bands between decks on certain double decked buses. These buses also had the 'F' prefix letter removed. (*Robert Dickson*)

This Alexander's Y-type Leyland Leopard, WXA935M (FPE35), is resting between runs on the local no. 86 service to Dunnikier Estate via Templehall Avenue. Kirkcaldy bus station was at the time going through the first of its refurbishments. (*Robert Dickson*)

YSF102S (FPE102) wears a variation of the 'large logo' applied to the Y-type Leopard. The lower half of the aluminium relief waist band has been removed, and it has the wide cream band but with an advert for Haig Whisky. The Haig adverts had been seen on Fife's buses for decades by this point in the mid-1980s. (*Robert Dickson*)

Mk 1 Volvo Ailsa LSX33P (RA33) is seen about to enter Glenrothes bus station wearing the experimental pre-'large logo' livery which was applied around the 1980–81 period. It should also be noted that vehicles wearing this livery variation also had the 'F' prefix removed from the fleet number. (*Paul Redmond*)

In the large logo days, the buses always seemed to look like they had a new lease of life, as shown here by Mk 2 Ailsa OSC59V (859). They looked fresher and brightened up the place with the wider cream band applied. The small white logo above the triangular destination panel seemed to be neither a standard nor non-standard application. (*Gordon Stirling*)

Mk 2 Ailsa OSC63V (FRA63) is caught travelling light from the Esplanade bus stance along the road, heading towards the depot. Having just terminated in Kirkcaldy on a service no. 6, it is likely that this was off on one of the short afternoon runs used by workers from Donibristle Industrial Estate at Dalgety Bay. (*Paul Redmond*)

Seen here approaching Kirkcaldy bus station from the west is former Y-type Leopard bus XXA854M (1054). It carried the fleet number FPE54 when new, and then became L12 when it was first converted before carrying its new number as pictured. Much use was often made of vehicles no longer required for service, many ending up as breakdown vehicles or training buses. (*Robert Dickson*)

OSC65V (RA65) was a Mk 2 Volvo Ailsa with the livery applied as described in a previous photograph. It will be noted that this vehicle has also had the 'F' prefix removed from the fleet number. It is seen entering Glenrothes bus station wearing a side advert for Wm Low superstore in Kirkcaldy. (*Paul Redmond*)

A rather busy Leyland Leopard, YSF85S (85), makes steady progress as it travels down Roxburgh Road in Glenrothes. It is seen on the no. 38 service to Kirkcaldy, having originated from Leslie, and will take in Thornton and Gallatown on its journey.

Leyland Olympian A987FLS (FRO7), with Alexander's R-type bodywork, is seen leaving Kirkcaldy with an in-house advertisement for the Glenrothes–Edinburgh interlink service. It has been added to a wide cream band that was being applied to certain vehicles around this time. (*Robert Dickson*)

Alexander's-bodied Leopard YSF97S (97) is seen wearing large logo livery in this view taken in 1988. It makes light work of the loadings as it departs Kirkcaldy on a busy run to Tanshall on service no. 38. (*Robert Dickson*)

Here we see Aberhill depot's Mk 1 Ailsa LSX39P (FRA39) as it is about to enter Kirkcaldy bus station on a service no. 5 from Bonnybank. This was a 2-hourly service which took in much of the Methil area before heading down the coast to Kirkcaldy. (*Robert Dickson*)

Alexander's-bodied Ailsa KSF1N was the first of its type to be delivered to an SBG company. Now numbered 801 and carrying its former owner Highland Scottish's red and grey livery, it was seen operating a local service at Glenrothes on 16 March 1993. New to Alexander's (Fife) as its FRA1 in July 1975, this historically important vehicle was subsequently preserved. (*Steve Vallance*)

The 'Large Logo' livery is well suited to this Alexander's P-type Leyland Tiger, D512CSF (412), as it leaves Kirkcaldy on the journey back to Ballingry. This route took in the Victoria Hospital, Chapel Village, Cardenden and Lochgelly. At one time, this route would have been run by Kirkcaldy depot, but by this time it was run from Cowdenbeath, going by the 'C' letter on the front of the bus. (*Robert Dickson*)

Kirkcaldy-based T-type Leyland Leopard NFS176Y (FPE176) is seen here departing from the town bus station in 1987 on a local no. 87 service to Chapel Village, to the north-west of the town. This was a circular anticlockwise route from the town centre and travelled via Templehall, Birnam Road, Chapel Village and Glamis Road before arriving back at the bus station. (*Robert Dickson*)

Kirkcaldy was the home to the first batch of Leyland Nationals, which arrived in Fife in 1978. They were 11.3m Mk 1 versions with roof mounted heater pods. On the left is HSC108T (FPN8) while sister vehicle HSC105T (FPN5) is on the right. These vehicles worked hard on the local routes around Kirkcaldy. (*Robert Dickson*)

YSF83S (FPE83) is seen on 16 August 1981, looking rather 'plain' as it leaves Kirkcaldy on a service no. 8 to Leven via the Toll Bar in Methil. I think the livery looked old fashioned and plain when the window pillars were left red. It seemed more in proportion when the pillars were painted cream. (*Robert Dickson*)

Posing for the camera at the layover area in Kirkcaldy bus station, we see Leyland Leopard CFS105S (FPE105) which has Duple Dominant Mk 1 bodywork. It had just arrived on the infrequent no. 36 service from Perth via Newburgh, its home port. This type of coach suited this run, which was almost a 2-hour journey. (*Robert Dickson*)

Leyland Leopard GSG128T (FPE128) is shown for comparison purposes and is seen here in the layover at Shorehead bus station, Leven. This coach has the Duple Dominant Mk 2 style of bodywork, which had a 'deeper' windscreen and driver's side window. (*Robert Dickson*)

A good study showing the differences in rear ends between the Mk 1, on the left, and the Mk 2 versions of the Leyland National. RSG842V (FPN24) shows the lack of decent ventilation for the engine compartment, leading to the manufacture of makeshift air intake vents for these vehicles, before Stagecoach arrived on the scene. The vehicle on the right is HSC101T (FPN1), Fife's first Leyland National. (*Robert Dickson*)

UFS877R (RA44) was one of the batch of Alexander's-bodied Mk 1 Ailsas that had these wide cream bands applied between decks and the 'F' prefix missing from the fleet number. This scheme was also applied to a batch of Fleetlines, and the fleet number change happened to new arrivals around this time too. I think the company was experimenting with liveries before the 'Large Logo' style happened in the mid-1980s. (*Paul Redmond*)

MCW Metrorider F70RFS (70) is seen here in Kirkcaldy bus station in the late 1980s on a day of local runs between the town centre and Harris Drive on the K6 service. These twenty-five-seat vehicles were new in 1988 and served around the Kirkcaldy area. (*Kenneth Barclay*)

Stagecoach Fife converted this vehicle, Leyland Titan WYV3T, into an exhibition unit to promote the 'New Deal', one of the government's initiatives for getting the unemployed back to work. The conversion was done in the workshops in Kirkcaldy in around 1998. (*David Beardmore*)

This Alexander's Y-type-bodied Leyland Leopard, TMS406X (206), arrived in 1992 from Ribble Buses along with half a dozen others. They were all originally Midland Scottish vehicles and were welcomed back by the older drivers who missed having a degree of control over their gear changing. (*Gordon Stirling*)

The MCW-bodied minibus, new in 1988, was practically a native of Kirkcaldy as I believe all twenty, bar one, served their time with the Fife company based in Kirkcaldy. F64RFS (64) is one example of these vehicles; it is seen between turns, sitting in the depot beside the wall near the roadside. (*John Law*)

Fife Scottish KSF6N (806) was looking very smart in Stagecoach candy stripe livery as it passed through Thornton bound for Glenrothes on 18 June 1994. Disappearing into the distance, bound for Kirkcaldy, is a Duple-bodied Leyland Leopard working for Moffat & Williamson, Glenrothes. (*Steve Vallance*)

K602ESH (602) was one of the Alexander's-bodied Dennis Darts that arrived in 1992. I think the Dart was more centred on Kirkcaldy, while the Volvo equivalent, the B6, was centred on Dunfermline. They were a good bus when they were new, but as time passed, the gearboxes tended to jump up and down between gears – very annoying, I can tell you. (*John Law*)

Jonckheere Mistral-bodied Volvo B10M articulated coach N561SJF (561) is seen here leaving Glasgow in 1998 as it starts its journey back to Anstruther. Two of these coaches arrived at Aberhill depot in 1996 for use on the long distance runs to Glasgow. They were sold on when the weight restriction was applied to Leven's Bawbee Bridge, making the buses effectively useless for their intended purpose. (*John Law*)

The first batch of Leyland Olympians ordered by Stagecoach after they bought the Fife Scottish company in 1991 included J808WFS (708). They were bodied by Alexander's with the 'RL' type. 708 would eventually find its way to United Counties, another of the Stagecoach subsidiary companies. (*Kenneth Barclay*)

Leyland Leopard YSF100S (100) nears the end of its journey as it approaches Glenrothes bus station in the early 1990s. The front end livery application, around the grille area, sadly lacked in imagination when applied to this particular vehicle. (*Steve Vallance*)

A general view looking to the northern end of Kirkcaldy bus station since its last redevelopment in 2007. It is a basic horseshoe-shaped layout with stances on the east and west sides. The layover for vehicles is tight into the central walled area. (*Allan Morton*)

This is the view of the southern end of Kirkcaldy bus station. When the bus station was remodelled, the pedestrian area was widened and it now looks a lot more open and spacious. The new waiting area, ticket office and drivers' room can be seen to good effect in this view. (*Allan Morton*)

Kirkcaldy depot got to try out a lot of demonstration buses in their day. Volvo B10L N141VDU (399) with Alexander's 'Ultra' low-floor bodywork is shown here. It is seen here after arrival from Falkirk in October 1995. It apparently never lasted long and ended up with First Glasgow. (*John Law*)

It is June 2002 at Glenrothes bus station, and we see an early Optare Solo belonging to Spencer of Leven beside two Fife Volvo Citybuses. The bus on the right is wearing the old candy stripe livery while B108CCS (15258), which was an ex-Volvo demonstrator, wears the new 'swirl' livery. (*Suzy Scott*)

A rather clean looking Leyland Tiger, D524DSX (424A) with Alexander's P-type bodywork belonging to Aberhill depot, has just arrived at Leven's Shorehead bus station in May 1992 on service no. 95 from St Andrews, further up the coast. (*Robert Dickson*)

One of the second-hand Leyland Titans acquired by Stagecoach in the mid-1990s is seen here in the layover area at Glenrothes bus station in July 2002. A834SUL (749) was new in 1983 to London Transport, but served well in the Fife fleet without too much trouble. Their only drawback was the fact they were a bit slow to drive. (*Suzy Scott*)

Representing one of Moffat & Williamson's modern fleet is Optare Solo MX06ADO. It is seen here within Glenrothes bus station, about to depart on service no. 5, one of their local routes around the Glenrothes area. (*John Law*)

Northern Counties-bodied Volvo Olympian N334HGK (16434) is seen in St Brycedale Road having passed the huge steeple of St Brycedale Church adjacent to the town's college as it makes its way down the road, heading for Kirkcaldy bus station. (*Michael Laing*)

Volvo Citybus C803USG (973) is about to depart from Glenrothes bus station on the service no. 36 to Perth. The date was July 2002, and it was not too long before the fleet number changed to 15273. The grey square on the front panel is the holding plate for the 'school bus' signs. (*Suzy Scott*)

In 2011, Stagecoach painted Alexander's Dennis Trident SP04DBV (18092 / FRT1AL) in this rendition of the old Ayres red and cream livery to commemorate the fiftieth anniversary of the formation of Alexander's (Fife) in 1961. Although seen here in Rosyth on a service no. 7 to Kirkcaldy, this is an Aberhill-based bus. (*Gordon Stirling*)

Alexander's PS-bodied Volvo B10 R338HFS (20338) is caught in a brief ray of sunshine while leaving Kirkcaldy on a miserable day in February 2011. It is heading back to Glenrothes on a service no. 39 via Newcastle (no, not that one). Only a few of these robust vehicles are left in Fife, this one having given fifteen years of sterling service. Much loved by Fife drivers. (*Gordon Stirling*)

Northern Counties-bodied Volvo Olympian R84XNO (16084) is pictured heading back towards the bus station, having come down the road on a local Kirkcaldy town service from the Dunnikier area to the north. Soon after this photograph was taken, this bus found itself transferred down the coast to Dunfermline depot. (*Gordon Stirling*)

A part view here of Glenrothes bus station showing the predominant statue which is named 'Ex Terra', which roughly translates to 'From the Earth'. Other people have referred to it as 'the family statue'. Glenrothes bus station is well situated in the heart of the new town, beside the Kingdom Shopping Centre.

There is an infamous low bridge in Kirkcaldy situated at the junction between Victoria Road and Dunnikier Road. Many double decked vehicles have been taken down Dunnikier Road by unsuspecting (new) drivers, resulting in the example shown here in March 2006, seen afterwards at the depot in Kirkcaldy. Luckily there have been no fatalities, as the buses have been out of service at the time. (*Nelson Ewan*)

Here we see Carlyle-bodied Dennis Dart H71MOB (A32347) of Aberhill depot, pulling out of its stance at Kirkcaldy bus station on a run to Mountfleurie in Leven on service no. 13C. I don't know why, maybe it's just me, but I always thought those vehicles looked like snow shovels or snow ploughs. (*Suzy Scott*)

One of Stagecoach Fife's new Alexander's-bodied MAN vehicles, SP08DDN (22580), is seen leaving Kirkcaldy bus station in March 2012 on an express service no. X26, where the ultimate destination will be Glasgow. Along with the Enviro 300 type buses, they are big enough to comfortably tackle inter urban duties, and, as seen here, are occasionally substituted for express service work. (*Chris Cuthill*)

Round about 2010, Stagecoach Fife bought some of these East Lancs-bodied Volvo B7s from their Strathtay counterparts. This example is SP51AWX (16923) and is seen passing the Adam Smith Theatre in Kirkcaldy, having come from Glenrothes via Thornton in February 2011. (*Gordon Stirling*)

Alexander's Dennis Enviro 400 SP60DRV (19661) is captured here about to head up the coast to Leven on the service no. 8. Alexander's-bodied 'R' type Volvo Olympian N850VHH (16850) is seen alongside and makes a good comparison of the progress in bodywork development by the Alexander's company. (*Gordon Stirling*)